T0005342

ACTION!

HOW MOVIES BEGAN

BY

MEGHAN McCARTHY

A Paula Wiseman Book
Simon & Schuster Books for Young Readers
NEW YORK LONDON TORONTO SYDNEY NEW DELHI

Movies. They take us on adventures, send us back in time, and introduce us to new people and places.

They allow us to peek into the life of the sixteenth-century's queen of England or step into the colorful excitement of the 1970s disco craze.

They can spark joy, sadness, and even fear. We can't imagine our world without them. When did movies start? Who invented them?

Elizabeth: The Golden Age, 2007

The evolution of the moving picture is a long journey, with many people adding a little bit of this and a little bit of that.

Saturday Night Fever, 1977

Throughout most of the 1800s, photography required considerably longer exposure times. Therefore, a freeze-frame photo of motion wasn't possible. Art such as this painting was the only way people could imagine a horse running, while frozen in time. The question is, did the artist get it right? Leland Stanford, a wealthy horse owner and once governor of California, didn't think so.

Leland Stanford

Based on a detail from the painting *The Hunt in Belvoir Vale* by John Ferneley Sr. and Sir Francis Grant, c. 1835

Even though by the 1870s camera exposure times had shortened, the question of what a horse's running gait looked like had not been answered. Stanford asked Eadweard Muybridge, who was a well-known nature photographer, to help him solve the mystery. How would a man who photographed stationary scenes, such as this valley, document something moving? Muybridge came up with a clever solution.

Eadweard Muybridge

Valley of the Yosemite from Union Point, 1872

Muybridge set up a row of cameras with threads that stretched across a track. When the horse broke the threads . . . SNAP! SNAP! SNAP! The cameras recorded a series of photos. This is one example. Does the horse look the same as the one in the painting?

The Horse in Motion, 1878

Muybridge's
photographs were inspired
by the motion experiments of a French
scientist named Étienne-Jules Marey. The two men met
while Muybridge was touring Paris in 1881. Marey wished to
record birds in flight, but Muybridge's technique didn't work well
with birds. Therefore, in 1882, Marey invented a handheld camera to
better record motion. The photographer had to pull the trigger in quick
succession to get results. These are a few of Marey's photographic studies.

Thomas Edison, the famous inventor, met with both Muybridge and Marey. Edison knew he could make a better invention than theirs. One of Edison's advantages was that he had a team of employees working for him. He assigned the project to inventor and photographer William Kennedy Dickson. After much work, Dickson came up with something called a Kinetograph, used to record motion, and a Kinetoscope, used to play back this motion. The motion was recorded on something called celluloid film. That's why movies are sometimes called films today. By 1893 the inventions were completed.

Below is what the inside of a Kinetoscope looks like.

Thomas Edison

William Kennedy Dickson

You can visit a Kinetoscope in a museum today! The one shown here is in West Orange, New Jersey, at Thomas Edison National Historical Park.

THE KINETOSCOPE PRESENTS THE BLACKSMITH SCENE

EDISON KINETOSCOPE

The Kinetograph was quite heavy, so it couldn't be transported outside. Therefore, Edison's team erected a building in which to use the new invention. When the men turned the crank, the roof opened.

When they pushed the building around the circular track, the roof and sun aligned, allowing sunlight to pour in and light up their films' subjects.

The Black Maria, named after a police wagon, 1893

Inside the Black Maria, Edison and his team created something magical. They created motion pictures.

William K. Dickson

One year later, the first Kinetoscope parlors opened. Inside these parlors, curious viewers peered into wooden boxes and watched slices of life animated for the first time.

This is what they saw . . .

"Carmencita," 1894
approximately 21 seconds long

"Fred Ott's sneeze," 1894
approximately 5 seconds long

"The Boxing Cats (Prof. Welton's)," 1894
approximately 20 seconds long

Brothers Auguste and Louis Lumière, whose family owned a large photography supply company in France, set out to invent a cheaper and lighter film camera. The Lumières thought watching films should be a group experience, so in addition to the camera, they invented a projector to share their films with the world.

Auguste AND *Louis Lumière*

Image based on the poster "Cinématographe Lumière," 1895

Their first public screening was in 1895. "We stared flabbergasted at this sight, stupefied and surprised beyond all expression," said a magician in the audience by the name of Georges Méliès. "At the end of the show there was complete chaos. Everyone wondered how such a result was obtained."

Here are some of the films shown that year. They are called the French word "*actualités*." They are something real, a slice of life. Cinema was born.

"Arrival of a Train at La Ciotat"

"Fishing for Goldfish"

"Baby's Meal"

"The Blacksmiths"

Back in the United States, Edison Manufacturing Co. created one of the first hand-tinted films, in 1895. It plays with movement and color.

Annabelle Serpentine Dance, 1895

The Serpentine Dance, 1897

After viewing the Lumière brothers' films, Georges Méliès couldn't resist buying his own film camera. It wasn't long before the magician figured out how to do magic tricks using the camera. In this two-minute film, he plays every role himself. What magic!

The One-Man Band, 1900

Méliès's most famous film is called *A Trip to the Moon.* By stopping the camera, placing a rocket ship in the moon's eye, and then restarting the recording, *POP!* a rocket ship appears to land with a splat. Méliès created a color version using the hand-painting techniques that Edison and the Lumières utilized.

A Trip to the Moon, 1902

As time went on, films got better. But something was missing—sound! Although this filmmaking time period was called the silent era, it was hardly silent. A pianist or even an orchestra would accompany the soundless films. Since the movies were silent, cards with hand-lettered type were cut into scenes, to communicate dialogue.

They looked like this . . .

Rebecca of Sunnybrook Farm, 1917

"I'm Emma Jane Perkins
and we've got <u>Seven</u> cows!"

The year was 1913. "We need some gags here," said a director to a young English-born Charlie Chaplin. "Put on comedy makeup. Anything will do." Chaplin said of his costume, "I wanted everything a contradiction: the pants baggy, the coat tight, the hat small and the shoes large." And just like that, one of the most memorable characters of the silent era was born.

Another actor named Buster Keaton was called a "stone-face comedian." Whatever happened around him, his expression never changed. "The more seriously I took my work," he once said, "the better laughs I got." Keaton's acrobatic skills and risk-taking make for jaw-dropping viewing, even to this day.

HOW-TO-BE
— A —
DETECTIVE

There were no special effects in the 1920s. In this scene Keaton did the stunt himself, no wires attached! He missed the building and fell into a net off-screen, badly bruising himself in the process.

Buster Keaton in *Three Ages*, 1923

Even today, some actors do their own stunts. Although Tom Cruise was attached to a wire, he missed the building and broke his ankle. Cruise and Keaton both illustrate a daring quality that makes them riveting to watch.

Tom Cruise on the set of *Mission: Impossible—Fallout*

Here you can see how one iconic movie scene inspired others.

Harold Lloyd in *Safety Last!*, 1923

Hugo, 2011

Back to the Future, 1985

In this scene, comedian Roscoe "Fatty" Arbuckle sticks forks into two dinner rolls and makes them dance.

Chaplin does the same thing.

The Rough House, 1917

The Gold Rush, 1925

Watch Johnny Depp do his own excellent rendition.

Benny & Joon, 1993

In the United States during what was called the Roaring Twenties, prejudice was quite apparent. People of color were rarely included in mainstream movies.

An African American actress by the name of Josephine Baker decided she'd had enough. She packed up her things and moved to France. "I felt liberated in Paris," she said. There she became a star!

Actresses like Baker, with her beauty, humor, and large stage presence, paved the way for the stars of today. In 2018 a Marvel movie titled *Black Panther*, with a majority black cast, was a smash hit. This is something Baker could have only dreamed of.

In 1925, the year that Josephine Baker moved to Paris, *The Phantom of the Opera* was released. During this time period, it was popular to use dyes to color parts of the films. *The Phantom of the Opera* effectively uses colors to create moody atmospheres using pinks, yellows, greens, and . . .

Americans weren't the only ones creating innovative films. *The Cabinet of Dr. Caligari* is thought to be the first full-length German horror film, released in 1920. It plays with light and shadow and lines. The world is angular, topsy-turvy, and jarring. The makeup is heavy and spooky. Shadows were hand-painted for dramatic effect.

In this scene all you can see is a person's shadow.

How does it make you feel?

Nosferatu, also created in Germany, is an early adaptation of the book *Dracula*. You can see how *The Cabinet of Dr. Caligari* was an inspiration. *Nosferatu* illustrates stop-motion techniques used by earlier filmmakers, such as Georges Méliès, for scenes in which doors open and close on their own. Haunting. Just the shadow of the vampire causes shivers.

Nosferatu, 1922

One of the earliest science fiction films that is still appreciated to this day is *Metropolis*. This futuristic German film remains relevant. In it, society's wealthy travel in flying vehicles and enjoy lavish garden parties while the low-paid workers suffer in a steam-filled underworld containing giant machines that must stay running 24/7. Some film critics loved it. Others hated it.

Regardless of the criticism, *Metropolis*'s innovative sets and costumes are a feast for the eyes.

Metropolis, 1927

The robot on the left is named C-3PO.

Does he look familiar?

Star Wars, 1977

This painting is inspired by *Metropolis*, 1927.

This painting is similarly inspired by *Blade Runner*, 1982.

Do you see the similarity?

One year after *Metropolis* was released, an all-talking movie called *Lights of New York* hit theaters. No one had watched a movie like this before! Imagine hearing your favorite actor speak for the first time. Imagine hearing city sounds for the first time—traffic, a crowd of people, the dings of a trolley car. What would you think? The sound in *Lights of New York* wasn't perfect, but people wanted more. Movie lovers began using the word "talkies," short for "talking movies," as in "I'm going to a talkie today."

One would think that all movies after *Lights of New York* would have sound, but that isn't so. Charlie Chaplin's last "silent" film opened in 1936, eight years after the first all-talking film had been released.

Lights of New York, 1928

Almost a century later, the movie *Lion*, which takes place in India, was released. In it you hear a train horn, hordes of people chattering and rushing this way and that, eerie chimes, and unintelligible announcements echoing through a concrete space. The sounds help illustrate the confusion and fear that Saroo, a young boy who is lost and wants to go home, is feeling. One movie inspires another, which inspires another.

Next time you watch a movie, think of all the people who tried something new and pushed the boundaries of what is possible. Movies will continue to inspire us for generations to come, and we have all the inventors, actors, writers, and directors to thank.

Lion, 2016

~Author's Note~

This book is not an extensive history of cinema's silent era. Instead, it is meant to be a jumping-off point, to get readers excited to learn more and hopefully do their own research by sampling old movies. Although this book is for children, I'm sure film buffs will wonder why I didn't include their favorite movies or genres. Due to the page count limitations and children's attention spans, my scope had to be very limited. Below are a few more interesting topics to dive into. Please visit my website for much more content on the silent movie era.

~ MGM's Leo the Lion ~

On this book's cover is one of MGM's lions being recorded for the iconic roar at the beginning of their movies. Although the mascot was always nicknamed Leo the Lion, there were in fact a handful of lions who filled this role. MGM's first lion was was named Slats, born in Ireland's Dublin Zoo, who made his debut in 1924. Since sound on film wasn't used yet, Slats's career remained a silent one on-screen. He was the only lion who did not roar. Jackie was the next lion to take over MGM's spot, and it's his story that is the most interesting. Jackie, also called Leo when publicized, had quite a number of brushes with death. The most bizarre incident happened when MGM put the lion on tour by both land and air. They built a cage into the back of a small monoplane. On the plane was painted the name "Leo" and below that was "MGM Flying Lion." In 1927, while flying from San Diego and on the way to New York, the plane's pilot, Martin Jensen, encountered severe storms. When he attempted to make an emergency landing, the plane hit a tree and crashed in the Arizona desert. Although the plane looked like a twisted piece of metal, Martin Jensen survived with only a "slight cut." He says this of what happened next:

> I crawled out to see what had happened to Leo. The cage was held tight and Leo wasn't scratched, but I'm here to tell you he looked disgusted . . . I figure his opinion of me as a flier is pretty low. When I asked him how he felt, he licked his chops and settled himself as best he could. I stripped a piece of aluminum from the plane and made a trough which I filled with water for him from a nearby creek. I fixed him up with what

milk we had left, divided my sandwiches with him and started down the canyon for help, not knowing where I was going. . . .

Papers also noted that the lion was "in an amiable mood" and made for a "splendid passenger." While the pilot wandered the desert in search of help, MGM announced that their pilot and lion were missing. Some newspapers wrote incredulous headlines such as MOVIE FIRM DENIES JENSEN FLIGHT HOAX. OFFICIALS SEARCH FOR PLANE CARRYING HIM AND LION. After walking for three days, according to papers, Jensen finally found help. He then led a search party to find the lion. One paper ran with the headline LION FOUND BUT MIGHTY HUNGRY.

After the survival story hit the news, Leo the Lion became "Leo the Lucky." Although I cannot verify this account, according to Mental Floss, Jackie aka Leo also "survived two train wrecks, an earthquake, a boat sinking, an explosion at the studio. . . ."

~ Female Editors ~

The phrase "cut to the chase," an expression that means hurry up and get to the point, originated from the silent movie era. During the early days of film, chase scenes were particularly popular sections of the movie, so cutting to the chase scene meant getting to the exciting part. Another silent era phrase is "on the

cutting room floor." This saying means that an idea was considered but ultimately discarded. In movie terms it means that a filmed scene was ultimately left out of the final picture. The "cut" part comes from the physical action of cutting films, leaving the parts not wanted on the "cutting room floor," and taping the rest back together. The job of cutting was often done by working-class women. One such woman was Margaret Booth. She started working as a cutter in 1915. Booth spoke of working in the early days of film, saying, "When you worked in the silent days, you learned about rhythm, and you learned to cut film like poetry." She remarked that if you "just learn to cut from sound, you can become choppy." In a Q&A in *Focus on Film*, Booth was asked how she got started:

> The studio said that when I finished school I could go to work there. I didn't know what that work meant. When I saw a film on the screen, I thought that's how it came out of the camera. I had no idea how it was put together. . . . When I was working in the lab, there were all young girls, all kids, really.

"How did you learn to cut?" the interviewer asked. "By watching," Booth said. She went on, saying,

> Mr. Stahl was the director and he cut his own pictures. He used to take me into the projection room. He would tell me why he went to a close-up. He said, "Always play it in the long shot unless you want to punctuate something." He told me the different techniques of cutting. And then at night I would stay until two or three in the morning and use the outtakes from the picture. I was practicing cutting with them, learning to do it on my own. And that's how I really learned to cut.

Booth was then asked, "Do you think people really understood the function of the film editor?" Booth replied, "No, no. I don't think anybody realizes how much film we have, how much film we have to handle." Then Booth remembered a specific film. "We had fifty thousand feet of film, with three cameras. And that's a lot of film to go through. . . . On *Mutiny on the Bounty*, when you have wrecks on the water and things like that, that have to be done over and over again, you have to go through it all. Much of it is useless, but then you get a little piece that's wonderful."

Margaret Booth worked as a cutter, an editor, supervising editor, and eventually executive producer. She didn't retire until the 1980s and held quite the résumé, working on films like *Annie* and *The Wizard of Oz*. She lived through an entire century, born in 1898 and died at the age of 104 in 2002. At the Academy Awards in 1978, she said, "I'm deeply grateful. But isn't it wonderful that one can win an award for something one loves to do? And I love my work."

~ The Beginnings of Hollywood ~

One could reasonably point to Thomas Edison as the catalyst for independent film studios fleeing New York to what was then called Hollywoodland. The letters of the sign were brought by men who "wearily plodded with each fragment of the sign strapped to their backs up the winding zig-zag path to the summit." The letters were then illuminated by thousands of light bulbs, which papers touted as a "gigantic electric sign, the largest in the world." The 1923 Hollywoodland sign was meant to advertise a real estate development. Little did the developer know he'd lure in something much greater—a mecca for film studios. To discover how this happened, one must go back to 1908.

Thomas Edison was what some would describe as a ruthless businessman.

One way he controlled his inventions was by way of the patent. When Edison couldn't be the first to invent something, he simply purchased the rights to the invention, as he did with his competitor's film projector, the Vitascope. In 1908, Edison convinced other competitors who held patents to join him in what was called the Motion Picture Patents Company, or what some called the Edison Trust. Edison even convinced Eastman Kodak, which was the largest producer of camera film, to join the patents company. Edison and his partners controlled the film cameras, the film projectors, and even the film! As a result, the trust had a virtual monopoly on all filmmaking and projecting. At every turn filmmakers were presented with lawsuits and forced to pay royalties to use the cameras and

film. Hundreds of lawsuits were filed. According to some, the trust even hired mobsters to rough people up when they stepped out of line.

The constant lawsuits slowed innovation down to a crawl. The scrappier among the independent creators did something bold. They got as far as possible away from Edison and his patents company, all the way to the other side of the country, to Hollywoodland. There, they were almost untouchable. After a litany of lawsuits, a 1915 ruling—*United States v. Motion Picture Patents Co.*—handed down a decision against the Motion Picture Patents Company, which delivered an almost fatal blow. The *New York Times* ran with a headline: ORDERS MOVIE TRUST TO BE BROKEN UP. The California filmmakers had won! From then on, the California filmmakers made innovative, longer pictures, while Edison's company was still creating shorts. Add great California weather to the mix, allowing filmmakers to film outside year-round, and Hollywood and movie-making magic became fully cemented in California.

~ The Disappearance of Louis Le Prince ~

Most people have never heard of Louis Le Prince. He was a Frenchman who studied physics and chemistry, worked as a photographer and painter, and bounced around between France, Britain, and the United States. He and his wife, Lizzie, set up an interior decoration firm in the US, and then Lizzie began teaching art at a school for the deaf in New York. The school allowed Le Prince to use their workshop facilities, and it was there that Le Prince first worked on his moving pictures camera. His first camera had sixteen lenses, and the patent for it was filed in 1886.

In 1887 Le Prince traveled back to Leeds, England, where he set up a workshop. "I'll keep you posted as I go," he wrote to his wife, who remained in New York with their children. "I'm getting nearer every day and now shall not leave it till done." Le Prince tried to keep his inventions secretive because he was afraid other would-be inventors would steal them. In Leeds, he developed a single-lens camera and made very brief moving images. Some theorize these were the first of their kind. Le Prince shot a very short scene of people walking in a circle, called "Roundhay Garden Scene." He also filmed his son playing the accordion as well as a street scene. Le Prince patented the single-lens camera and projector in the US in 1888.

Le Prince was competing against other inventors to create the first motion picture camera, Thomas Edison among them, although Edison and the others were years behind. After more experimentation Le Prince planned his momentous trip back to New York City. It was there that he planned to show the world something very special. Le Prince's wife found a venue for him to present his invention to New Yorkers at the Jumel Mansion. But before Le Prince was to sail off, he needed to discuss some family business with his brother in France. He was to travel by steam train to Paris. Once there he would first meet up with friends. The book *The Missing Reel* begins this way:

> He left Dijon for Paris on Tuesday, September 16, 1890. He missed the morning train. After an early lunch Albert accompanied him in a cab to the station. They arrived early to be on the safe side. Albert waited to see him off on the 2:42 pm. They chatted warmly to each other on the platform. They had managed to discuss the will over lunch. To Le Prince's relief it had all seemed very straightforward. Albert assured him that he would receive his share of the inheritance within months. Neither he nor Le Prince noticed the man in the brown coat watching them from the opposite platform.

That is quite the ominous beginning. Le Prince's friends never saw their friend the inventor again. Le Prince had vanished without a trace. Not only was Le Prince gone, but so was his luggage. There was no indication of where he went or why. As the years passed, all sorts of conspiracy theories have developed regarding Le Prince's disappearance. Some theorize that he committed suicide due to money troubles. Le Prince's wife had a far more sinister theory, that Thomas Edison arranged for Le Prince to disappear. Because Le Prince vanished without ever presenting his films to the world, he did not influence future filmmakers and would not go down in history like Edison or the Lumières as one of the originators of the moving picture.

~ Makeup in the Silent Era ~

In the early days of the silent era, film stars wore heavy makeup and made use of some very odd colors. Much of the film of the time period was blue sensitive, which meant red, orange, and yellow tones appeared almost black, and blue tones like a blue sky and even blue eyes appeared almost white. Skin tones looked darker and any blemishes were more noticeable. Freckles apparently filmed black. For this reason, film stars had become adept at imagining themselves in this black-and-white world. Some film directors and actors peered through blue glass filters to give them a better sense of what the final product would look like. "When seen in the sunlight, the makeup of the motion picture actor presents a most ghastly appearance," wrote one movie-making book in 1914. "Be very sparing in the use of lip rouge. Remember that red photographs black and that a heavy application of rouge shows an unnaturally black mouth on screen," warned a book from 1920. The book from 1914 stated,

> In nearly all cases the face is first thoroughly whitened and then tinted with yellow so that any subsequent color that may be applied

will stand out in bold relief, and also for the reason that the face will appear white instead of gray, as would be the case with the natural color of the complexion. The lips and the area surrounding the eyes are tinted with a color having a bluish cast such as heliotrope or mauve.

Actresses, however, were warned not to overdo it. A book from 1920 stated, "Some actresses think that the lighter they can make themselves, the more youthful they appear, whereas they only succeed in making themselves look like billiard balls." Men as well as women wore heavy makeup, often circling their eyes with dark coloration, looking semi-racoonish on film.

A contributor to the magazine *Bustle* tried out the colors for herself, using theater greasepaint and going by a guide from the 1920s. "The guide calls for bluish tones on the forehead, bluish on the cheeks, and blue under the eyes. On film, this is the first step to give your face dimension. In real life, you look like Smurfette's child. . . ."

~ Selected Bibliography ~

FILMS/TV/VIDEO

Andersen, Thom, Fay Andersen, and Morgan Fisher, dirs. 1975. *Eadweard Muybridge, Zoopraxographer.* New Yorker Films.
Brownlow, Kevin, and David Gill, dirs. 1987. *Buster Keaton: A Hard Act to Follow.* Thames Television.
Cinema's Birth to Modern Day—A Timeline of World Cinema. YouTube. Ministry of Cinema, November 4, 2017. https://youtu.be/xzHX4K8_Epk.
Cousins, Mark, dir. 2012. *The Story of Film. An Odyssey—Part 1.* Hopscotch Films.
Crash Course: Film History. YouTube. PBS Digital Studios, 2017. https://youtu.be/avAALYc7jw8.
Ferrari, Michelle, dir. 2015. *Edison, The Father of Invention.* https://www.imdb.com/name/nm0274109/?ref_=tt_ov_dr.
"Margaret Booth Receives an Honorary Award: 1978 Oscars." Oscars, February 4, 2016.
"One Hundred Years of Cinema." YouTube, 2016. https://www.youtube.com/c/onehundredyearsofcinema/videos.
Wilkinson, David, dir. 2016. *The First Film.* Guerilla Films.

BOOKS

Adam, Hans Christian. *Eadweard Muybridge: The Human and Animal Locomotion Photographs.* Germany: Taschen, 2010.
Chaplin, Charlie. *My Autobiography.* London: The Bodley Head, 1964.
Crafton, Donald. *The Talkies: American Cinema's Transition to Sound 1926–1931.* University of California Press, 1997.
Dickson, W. K. L. *History of the Kinetograph, Kinetoscope, and Kinetophonograph.* New York: Arno Press, 1970.
Koszarski, Richard. *An Evening's Entertainment: The Age of the Silent Feature Picture, 1915–1928.* Berkeley, CA: University of California Press, 1990.
Marta, Braun. *Picturing Time: The Work of Etienne-Jules Marey (1830–1904).* Chicago: University of Chicago Press, 1992.
Muybridge, Eadweard. *The Attitudes of Animals in Motion, Illustrated with the Zoopraxiscope.* London: W. M. Clowes and Sons, 1882.
Musser, Charles. *The Emergence of Cinema: The American Screen to 1907.* Berkeley, CA: University of California Press, 1990.
Nowell-Smith, Geoffrey. *The Oxford History of World Cinema.* Oxford: Oxford University Press, 1996.
Orthochromatic Photography. Rochester, NY: Eastman Kodak Company, 1919.
Rawlence, Christopher. *Missing Reel.* London: Collins, 1990.

ARTICLES/JOURNALS

"Another Unit in Hollywoodland Is Opened." *Los Angeles Evening Press,* December 8, 1923.
Associated Press. "Jensen Tells Story of Mountain Crash; Lion Escapes Injury." *Honolulu Star-Bulletin,* September 20, 1927.
Atkins, Irene Kahn. "Margaret Booth." *Focus on Film:* Vol. 25, 1975.
Dachille, Arielle. "I Tried a Vintage Film Star Makeup Tutorial." *Bustle,* July 5, 2014.

Eagan, Daniel. "A Trip to the Moon as You've Never Seen It Before: One of the Landmark Films in Cinema Can Now Be Seen in Color." *Smithsonian Magazine,* September 2, 2011.
Eschner, Kat. "The Story of Hollywood's Most Famous Lion." *Smithsonian Magazine,* April 17, 2017.
"Film Editors Hold Most Important Place in Movie Industry." *Dayton Daily News,* January 23, 1938.
Gil, Alexandra. "Breaking the Studios: Antitrust and the Motion Picture Industry." *NYU Journal of Law & Liberty,* 2008.
"Ground Is Broken for Mulholland Highway." *Los Angeles Evening Express,* December 15, 1923.
Heller, Steven. "The Font That Speaks for Silent Film." *Atlantic,* July 10, 2014.
Holiday, Harmony. "A Dinner in France, 1973: Josephine Baker, James Baldwin, and a Very Young Henry Louis Gates, Jr." *Lit Hub,* March 11, 2021.
"Huge Electric Sign Blazons Name of District Across Sky." *Los Angeles Evening Express,* December 8, 1923.
"Jensen Finds Leo at Plane." *Tampa Times,* September 22, 1927.
"Lion Found but Mighty Hungry." *Greenwood Commonwealth,* September 22, 1927.
"Monoplane of Dole Flight Fame Is Reported Missing." *North Adams Transcript,* September 19, 1927.
"Movie Firm Denies Jensen Flight Hoax." *Boston Globe,* September 19, 1927.
Muybridge, J. "The Horse in Motion." *Nature,* 1882.
Myrent, Glenn. "When Movies Began and No One Came." *New York Times,* December 29, 1985.
Newby, Richard. "The Quiet Horror of 'Nosferatu the Vampyre' at 40." *Hollywood Reporter,* October 12, 2019.
"Orders Movie Trust to Be Broken Up." *New York Times,* October 2, 1915.
Shimamura, Arthur P. "Muybridge in Motion: Travels in Art, Psychology and Neurology." *History of Photography,* 2002.
Sinha-Roy, Piya, and Jill Serjeant. "Tom Cruise Breaks Ankle, Shutting Down 'Mission: Impossible 6'." *Reuters,* August 16, 2017.
Youngs, Ian. "Louis Le Prince, Who Shot the World's First Film in Leeds." *BBC News,* June 23, 2015.
Yumbi, Joshua. The Phantasmagoria of the First Hand-Painted Films." *Nautilus,* July 16, 2015.

WEBSITES

Bennet, James. Cosmetics and Skin "Early (Silent) Movie Make-up"
http://www.cosmeticsandskin.com/cdc/early-movie.php.

RADIO

"Buster Keaton Discusses Release When Comedy Was King." Buster Keaton interviewed by Studs Terkel, aired September 5, 1960. https://studsterkel.wfmt.com/programs/buster-keaton-discusses-release-when-comedy-was-king.

LIST OF FILMS REFERENCED IN THIS BOOK

(Color indicates film rating or author's determination G, PG, PG-13, R, not rated.)
Films 1968 and beyond are rated by the MPAA. Films before that are by author's assessment.

Annabelle Serpentine Dance. 1895.

The Arrival of a Train at La Ciotat. Auguste Lumière & Louis Lumière, dirs. Lumière, 1896.

Baby's Meal. Auguste Lumière & Louis Lumière, dir. Lumière, 1895.

Back to the Future. Robert Zemeckis, dir. Universal Pictures, 1985.

Benny & Joon. Jeremiah S. Chechik, dir. MGM, 1993.

Black Panther. Ryan Coogler, dir. Marvel Studios, 2018.

The Blacksmiths. Auguste Lumière & Louis Lumière, dirs. Lumière, 1895.

Blade Runner. Ridley Scott, dir. The Ladd Company, 1982.

The Boxing Cats (Prof. Welton's). William K. L. Dickson. Edison Manufacturing Company, 1894.

The Cabinet of Dr. Caligari. Robert Weine, dir. Decla-Bioscope AG, 1920.

Carmencita. William K. L. Dickson, dir. Edison Manufacturing Company, 1894.

Elizabeth: The Golden Age. Shekhar Kapur, dir. Universal Pictures, 2007.

Fred Ott's Sneeze. William K. L. Dickson, dir. Edison Manufacturing Company, 1894.

Fishing for Goldfish. Auguste Lumière & Louis Lumière, dirs. Lumière, 1895.

The Gold Rush. Charles Chaplin, dir. Charles Chaplin Productions, 1925.

Hugo. Martin Scorsese, dir. Paramount Pictures, 2011.

Lights of New York, Bryan Foy, dir. Warner Bros., 1928.

Lion. Garth Davis, dir. The Weinstein Company, 2016.

Metropolis. Fritz Lang, dir. Universum Film AG, 1927.

Mission Impossible—Fallout. Christopher McQuarrie, dir. Paramount Pictures, 2018.

Nosferatu. F.W. Murnau. Jofa-Atelier Berlin-Jhannisthal, dir. 1922.

The One-Man Band, 1900.

Rebecca of Sunnybrook Farm. Marshall Neilan, dir. Mary Pickford Company, 1917.

The Rough House. Roscoe "Fatty" Arbuckle & Buster Keaton, dirs. Comique Film Company, 1917.

Safety Last! Fred C. Newmeyer & Sam Taylor, dirs. Hal Roach Studios, 1923.

Saturday Night Fever. John Badham, dir. Paramount Pictures, 1977.

Star Wars. George Lucas, dir. Lucusfilm, 1977.

Three Ages. Edward F. Cline, dir. Buster Keaton Productions, 1923.

A Trip to the Moon. Color version, 1902.

SIMON & SCHUSTER BOOKS FOR YOUNG READERS

An imprint of Simon & Schuster Children's Publishing Division • 1230 Avenue of the Americas, New York, New York 10020

© 2022 by Meghan McCarthy • Book design by Chloë Foglia © 2022 by Simon & Schuster, Inc.

Buster Keaton image is used by permission The Granger – Historical Picture Archive.

The photos of Studios of Union Film, Berlin; Hollywood Land; and MGM Lion images used by permission of GETTY IMAGES, Inc.

Berlin: ullstein bild Dtl./ullstein bild/Getty Images. • Hollywood Land: Underwood Archives/Getty Images. • MGM Lion: Jonathan Kobol Foundation/Movie Pix/Getty Images.

All rights reserved, including the right of reproduction in whole or in part in any form.

SIMON & SCHUSTER BOOKS FOR YOUNG READERS and related marks are trademarks of Simon & Schuster, Inc.

For information about special discounts for bulk purchases, please contact Simon & Schuster Special Sales at 1-866-506-1949 or business@simonandschuster.com.

The Simon & Schuster Speakers Bureau can bring authors to your live event. For more information or to book an event,

contact the Simon & Schuster Speakers Bureau at 1-866-248-3049 or visit our website at www.simonspeakers.com.

The text for this book was set in Rockwell • The illustrations for this book were rendered in acrylic paint.

Manufactured in China• 0423 SCP

2 4 6 8 10 9 7 5 3

Library of Congress Cataloging-in-Publication Data

Names: McCarthy, Meghan, author.

Title: Action! : how movies began / Meghan McCarthy.

Description: First edition. | New York : A Paula Wiseman Book, Simon & Schuster Books for Young Readers, 2022. | Includes bibliographical references. |

Audience: Ages 4-8 | Audience: Grades 2-3 | Summary: "Meghan McCarthy tells the story of the history of movies and the creators who made them.

In fascinating detail, she shows how early photography capturing motion became silent films, which led to the first color films"— Provided by publisher.

Identifiers: LCCN 2021008188 (print) | LCCN 2021008189 (ebook) | ISBN 9781534452305 (hardcover) | ISBN 9781534452312 (ebook)

Subjects: LCSH: Motion pictures—History—Juvenile literature.

Classification: LCC PN1993.5.A1 M423 2022 (print) | LCC PN1993.5.A1 (ebook) | DDC 791.4309—dc23

LC record available at https://lccn.loc.gov/2021008188 • LC ebook record available at https://lccn.loc.gov/2021008189